Goo

First
Politically
Corrupt
Dictionary

Dan Goodman

abreast *(a brest)* what Gov. Christine Todd Whitman could make if she pushed her two together

abridge *(e brij)* what Ted Kennedy sometimes drives off of

abroad *(e brôd)* how Bob Packwood refers to a woman

absolute *(ab se loot)* the vodka most senators prefer in their martinis

abstain *(ab stan)* a spot on Clinton's stomach after a trip to the buffet

abyss *(e bis)* what a drunken politician says he takes in the bathroom " 'Scuse me boys, I ... I gotta go take abyss"

accountable *(e kount e bel)* what a good politician never is for his actions

5

accountant *(e kount nt)* a person who helps you cover up the money stolen from taxpayers

address *(ad res)* an article of clothing once worn by J. Edgar Hoover

adore *(e dor)* what Gerald Ford often walks into

advisor *(as viz er)* a person who is paid to tell a President what everyone else tells him for free

affirmative action *(e fur me tiv ak shen)* a process by which minorities can be laid off and fired just as easily as everyone else

affordable *(e fôr de bel)* something that can be charged to your government expense account

agenda *(e jen de)* how Senators from the deep south differentiate the sexes

air space *(âr spas)* anything inside a politician's head

allies *(al iz)* any country which, in a time of war, doesn't want us to kick their ass

amass *(a mas)* the best way to describe President Clinton's gut

anonymous *(e non e mes)* that guy who Ross Perot picked to be his Vice President

arms reduction *(ärmz ri duk shen)* what Bob Dole suffered as a result of WWII

assets *(as etz)* the backup staff of a political ass

back tax *(bak taks)* a tax paid by
  a prostitute

best-case scenario *(best Kas si nâr
  eo)* a scenario in government which
  rarely comes true

Bill of Rights *(Bil of Ritz)* the rights that
  everyone believes in having while
  also believing not everyone should
  have them

bills *(bilz)* what The President signs
  and what everyone else pays

birth control *(bûrth ken trol)*
  a) an effective means of controlling procreation
  b) Janet Reno's face

black tie *(blk ti)* what you might have if Jesse Jackson and Clarence Thomas got into a race

blowhard *(blo hard)* what some congressional pages do to get ahead

blue collar *(bloo kol er)* what Hoover often wore to match his blue panties

bonus *(bo nes)* what most politicians do after we vote for them

boycott *(boi kot)* what gay politicians keep in their office

boys club *(boiz klub)* a club Janet Reno could probably get into

bribe *(brib)* an unsolicited donation

budget *(buj it)* a series of numbers which, when added, always yield a different result

bureaucrat *(byoo e krat)* one who excels in making simple things difficult

cabinet *(kab e nit)* where Senators from Massachusetts hide their liquor

campaign *(kam pan)* a series of stops made by a politician to see the states they will eventually ignore

carpet *(kar pit)* what Newt Gingrich doesn't want to believe his sister munches

censorship *(sen ser ship)* a process of xxxxx in which xxxxx are xxx xxxx see

cent *(sent)* a) a unit of money b) how Bob Packwood tracks down women

change *(chanj)* what honest tax payers are left with after honestly paying their taxes

character *(kar ik ter)* what politicians say their opponents don't have but go ahead and attack anyway

circle *(sur kel)* what angry citizens do to the heads of politicians they hope to assassinate

clue *(kloo)* what politicians never have but always seem to leave behind

collapse *(ke laps)* when 2 politicians have the same lapse in judgment

comeback *(kum bak)* what congressmen ask their receptionists to do after everyone else has gone home

common sense *(kom en sens)* sense in Washington that isn't very common

Communism *(Kom ye niz em)* a system of government where everyone gets shafted equally

confetti *(ken fet e)* a government document that is no longer incriminating. "When asked to present the files her boss had used, Fawn Hall produced a pile of confetti."

confidential *(kon fi den shel)* incriminating

congressional seat *(ken gresh en l set)* what congressmen spend most of their time sitting on

conservation *(kon ser va shen)* a process of keeping something until you can make more friends by getting rid of it

consequence *(kon si kwens)* the order in which a politician's cons take place

context *(kon tekst)* what every politician's quotes are always taken out of

contribution *(kontre byoo shen)* something most politicians accept but never seem to make in return

crackpot *(krak pot)* two things Marion Barry thinks are good on a buffet

crime *(krim)* anything you're caught doing that you can't bribe your way out of

crisis *(kri sis)* a situation which, if ignored long enough, will be handled by someone else

dark horse *(dark hors)* what Steve Forbes and Ross Perot bought their daughters for their 8th birthdays

debate *(di bat)* an open discussion between two opponents to see who can offend the least amount of people

debt limit *(det lim it)* something the national debt apparently doesn't have

Declaration of Independence *(Dek le ra shen of In di pen dens)* what Marion Barry gave after coming out of rehab

deliver *(di liv er)* what politicians are betting will die first on Ted Kennedy

17

demand *(di mand)* what gay military personnel are if caught in the act of love

democracy *(di mok re se)* a government for the people by a few people who don't give a crap about all the other people

Democrat *(Dem e krat)* someone who makes decisions as if they were an ass

deposit *(di poz it)* what Gary Hart left in Donna Rice

details *(de talz)* small important issues which are ignored as often as big important issues

dictator *(dik ta ter)* a foreign object on a politician's penis. "When JFK came home after a roll in the hay with Marilyn, Jackie saw a dictator hanging off his penis."

18

dirt *(durt)* something good as long as it's about someone else

dole *(dol)* to be old, out of touch, or in need of a hand

down pat *(doun pat)* a) something learned or mastered perfectly b) where Pat Buchanan likes his wife to go

down size *(doun siz)* what Rush Limbaugh can't do to his trousers

driller *(dril er)* what most politicians want to do to their secretaries

drug free school *(drug fre skool)* what the school would be after Marion Barry went through it

earned income *(ûrnd in kum)* income politicians don't work hard to earn

economic boom *(ek e nom ik boom)* the sound the economy will make when it eventually crashes

election *(i lek shen)* what some Asian politicians can't keep in their pants

equality *(i kwol i te)* something that everyone wants except with those people less fortunate than themselves

exit poll *(eg zit pol)* what Pat Buchanan might say to an unwanted Polish visitor

experience *(ik spere ens)* what people think is needed to turn Washington around even though it's responsible for getting Washington where it is

face *(fas)* a distinguishing feature which politicians have two of

facedown *(fac down)* the best way to look at Janet Reno

favor *(fa ver)* what politicians do for politicians but not for the people who elected them

fence *(fens)* what politicians must learn to walk if they hope to get elected

First Lady *(Furst La de)* the woman who took the President's virginity

flat tax *(flat taks)* a tax that women with small breasts have to pay

foreign affairs *(for in e fars)* what spies engage in to get information

foreign currency *(for in kur en se)* what politicians exchange their kickbacks into

forums *(fôr emz)* what politicians say when they don't know what something is for

framework *(fram wûrk)* what political spies do to get rid of an opponent

free election *(fre il ek shen)* an election candidates spend millions of dollars to win

free lunch *(fre lunch)* what politicians say there's no such thing as but always seem to get

free ride *(fre rid)* what the President always gets on Air Force One

freedom *(fre dem)* an American's right to do as he/she chooses provided the government says it's okay

funds *(fundz)* who Strom Thurmond thinks was that cool guy on "Happy Days"

Gerald Ford *(jer ald ford)* the reason
Betty Ford drank

getaway *(get a wa)* a common
phrase between Anita Hill and
Clarence Thomas

"go for the throat" *(go for the throt)*
what JFK does in the Zapruder film

GOP *(G O P)* Greedy Old Pricks

GOPAC *(go pak)* what Bill Clinton told George Bush after he won the election

government *(guv ern ment)* a group of people with one single goal who can't agree on one single thing

grass roots *(gras rootz)* the part of the grass the president did not inhale

gross *(gros)* a) any revenue before taxation b) the thought of seeing Strom Thurmond naked

gross income *(gros in kum)* the income of politicians considering what they accomplish

gun control *(gun kon trol)* what James Brady wishes John Hinkley had

Hail to the Chief *(hal to the chef)* what many angry citizens would like to throw

hangover *(hang o ver)* what you can see Rush Limbaugh's gut do to his belt

homeless *(hom lis)* what the President is when he is having an affair

honest *(on lis)* what most politicians would be if they weren't so busy lying

honor *(on er)* a) integrity in one's own beliefs or actions   b) where Paula Jones said Bill Clinton wanted to be

hope *(hop)* the feeling you lose three months after an election

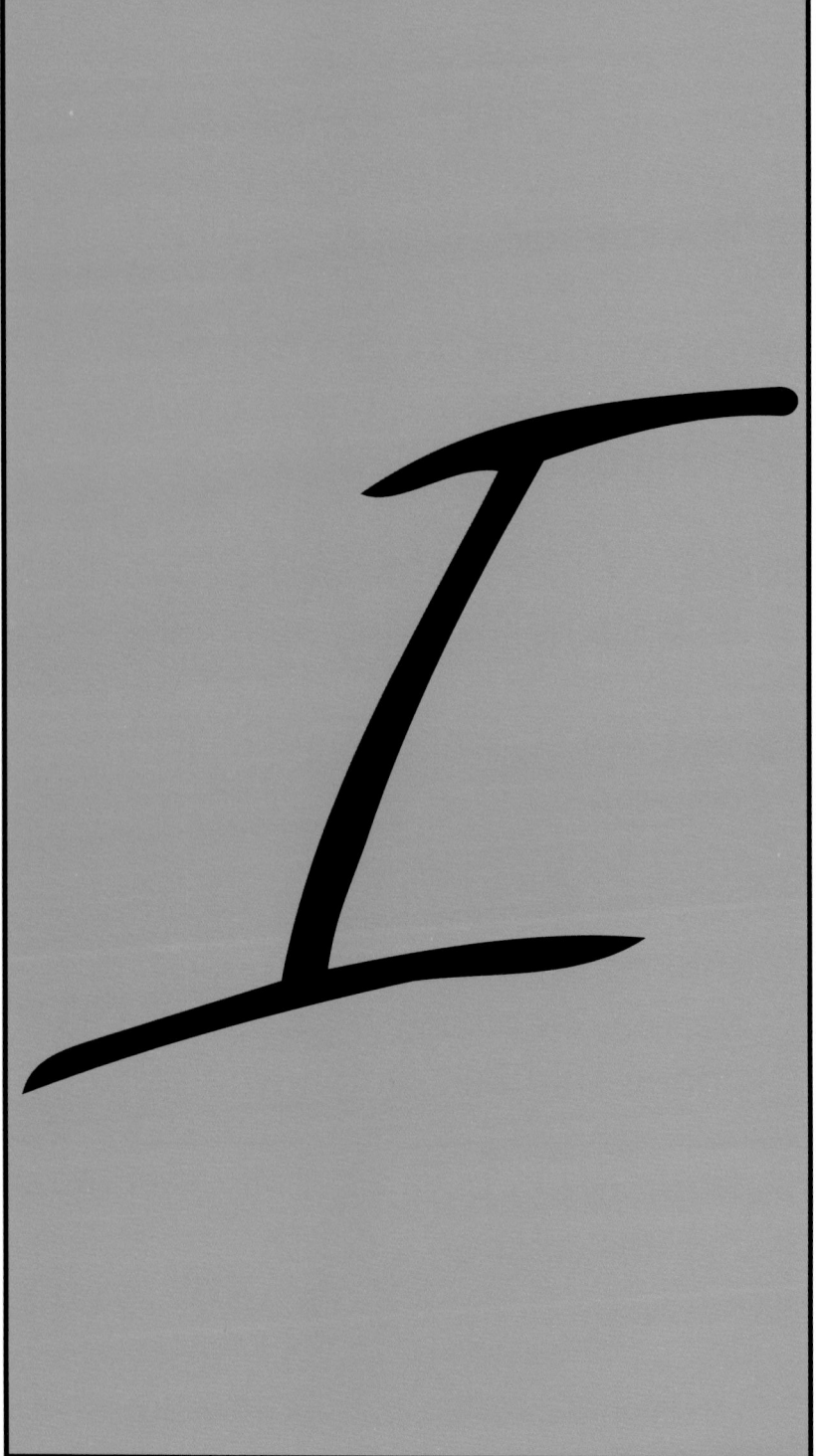

ideology *(i de ol ege)* the study of why politicians can never have an original idea

illegal aliens *(i le gal ale en)* politician's housekeepers and gardeners

improper *(im prop er)* a type of accounting method

inaugural ball *(in ô gyer el bal)* the first time the President has sex in the White House

income *(in kum)* how JFK fantasized about Marilyn Monroe

inflation *(in fla shen)* a phenomena which happens to everything but your paycheck

information *(in for ma shen)* how politicians arrange their lies so they appear more believable

insider *(in si der)* where Gennifer Flowers claims Bill Clinton was

intellect *(in tl ekt)* the thing which separates normal people from those who want to go into politics

interest *(in ter ist)* the feeling politicians have in nothing but themselves

interview *(in ter vyoo)* one question asked 30 different ways by 30 different people getting 30 different responses

invest *(in vest)* where Marion Barry likes to keep his crack

irrelevant *(i rel e vent)* anything said by the Vice President

isolate *(i so lat)* the first word uttered by a tardy Italian Head of State. "Isolate for this meeting! I'm a so sorry!"

issues *(ish ooz)* public concerns which are avoided at all costs

jacket *(jak it)* what politicians always do to the price of living

jail bait *(jal bat)* the type of girl Rob Lowe doesn't hope to meet at the next Democratic Convention

janitor *(jan i ter)* the only White House job Michael Dukakis <u>was</u> qualified for

job *(job)* what someone who doesn't work for the federal government has

Joint Chiefs *(joint chefs)* what Al Gore and Tommy Lee Jones were in college

joke *(jok)* Fritz Mondale

joy *(joi)* who Bob Packwood feels after feeling Merry

judo *(joo do)* what David Duke swears he will never eat

keg *(keg)* what you'll often find empty at the Kennedy compound

keno *(ke no)* a) a game of chance b) the only two English word Zoë Baird's housekeeper understood

KGB *(ka ge be)* Dan Quayle's favorite letters to guess when he plays 'Wheel of Fortune'

kick-back *(kik bak)* what FDR couldn't do if you kicked him

39

lame duck *(lam duk)* the entree at $500 a seat fundraising dinners

layoff(s) *(la ôf)* how male politicians decide which girl will be their secretary

leak *(lek)* what inside sources are busy giving while politicians are busy taking

liability *(li e bil ite)* one's ability to
    lie believably

liberal *(lib er el)* what every politician is
    with his/her promises

Lincoln Log *(lin con log)* what
    Abraham Lincoln left in the toilet

liquid paper *(lik wid pa per)* what the
Clinton's wish their Whitewater
documents were made of

long term plan *(lông tûrm plan)* a plan
in which your successor will have to
deal with all of your mistakes

loophole *(loop hol)* what politicians
always find before they're found out

mandate *(man dat)* what officers hide under the "don't ask - don't tell" policy

margin *(mä jin)* what Ted Kennedy says his martinis need

Median Family Income *(me de an fam le in kum)* those incomes from which the majority of taxes are derived

MediCare/MedicAid *(med i kâr / med í kad)* insurance programs that cover everyone but the people paying for them

message *(mes ij)* what politicians always have but never seem to get

middle class *(mid l klas)* those citizens neither wealthy enough nor poor enough to receive special attention from the government

military *(mil i ter e)* a group of people who end up protecting foreigners more than Americans

minimum wage *(min e mem waj)* the lowest hourly rate guaranteed by the government which is never enough to live on ... guaranteed

minority whip *(mi nôr i te wip)* what David Duke has fantasies of being able to use

misjudge *(mis juj)* what no one would do if Clarence Thomas died

moderate *(mod er it)* what Ted Kennedy likes to think his liver disease is

morale *(me ral)* how Alfonse D'Amato refers to his genitals

mud slinging *(mud sling ing)* an activity much more entertaining when done by naked women in a strip club

nationwide *(na shen wid)* what the Indians said before we stole all their land

NATO *(Nato)* Dan Quayle's first words when told he would be Vice President. George Bush - "Dan, how would you like to be Vice President?" Dan Quayle - "Nato!!"

negotiation *(ni go she a shen)* a process in Washington where both sides claim to have gotten exactly what they wanted

New Deal *(noo del)* what Marion Barry negotiates when his crack prices get too high

newt *(noot)* a disgusting, slimy creature which, if not controlled, may one day destroy mankind

nominee *(nom e ne)* that individual who spends the most money on negative ads

non-partisan *(non pärti zen)* to hate and distrust all politicians equally

O *(oµ)* the letter Dan Quayle adds to words when there isn't room for an E

offer *(ô fer)* what Bill Clinton would often like to do to Hillary

outsider *(out si der)* what Socks the cat is since there's no litter box in the White House

outspoken *(out spo ken)* what Dan Quayle could be by a six year old

Packwood *(pak wood)* what most politicians say they do in their pants

party lines *(pär te linz)* what Marion Barry says he doesn't do anymore

peanuts *(pe nutz)* a) nuts that Jimmy Carter would sometimes try to grow b) a comic strip that Dan Quayle could sometimes understand

pen pal *(pen pal)* an affectionate nickname for Bob Dole's right hand

penniless *(pen i lis)* what a dollar will probably be worth tomorrow in relation to what it's worth today

Pentagon *(Pent e gon)* a 5-sided building which gives at least 5 sides to every story

phone bill *(fon bil)* what Gennifer Flowers could do after Hillary had fallen asleep

platform *(plat form)* a kind of shoe found in J. Edgar Hoover's closet

policies *(pol e sez)* guidelines set by politicians that politicians never follow

political movement *(pe lit I kel moov ment)* what politicians have in the bathroom

poll *(pol)* a means of surveying never trusted unless it says you're ahead

pork barrel *(pork bar el)* what Bob Packwood would do if the barrel had breasts

positive *(poz i tiv)* how most people feel when asked if the government is lying to them

pot-shots *(pot shotz)* what Bill Clinton swears he never took

power tie *(pou er ti)* what politicians use when engaging in rough sex

President *(prez i dent)* someone who receives welfare even though he has a job

press *(pres)* what politicians prefer to deal with on the back nine of a golf course

prevent *(pri vent)* the era before vents were used to eavesdrop on conversations

primary *(pri mer e)* what Ted Kennedy didn't even try to do when his car went into Chappaquidik

private sector *(pri vit sek ter)* the area of a woman Bob Packwood often touched

pro-choice *(pro chois)* supporting a woman's right to choose unless she chooses to become pro-life

pro-life *(pro lif)* to support the rights of unborn children until they are born and no longer your concern

programs (pro gramz) the way Marion Barry likes his drugs to be purchased

public housing *(pub lik hou zing)* housing the majority of the public pays for and the majority of the public can't live in

quarter *(kwôr ter)* a) a unit of money
b) the amount of room left in the
bed after Rush Limbaugh gets in it

question *(kwes chen)* what politicians
prefer to do rather than answer

questionnaire *(kwes che nâr)* what
Dan Quayle used to do since he
couldn't see air

"Read my lips" *(Red mi lipz)* what Barbara Bush says to George when she's in the mood for sex

rebut *(ri but)* what conservative Republicans don't want gay men to do

record *(rek erd)* what politicians would rather listen to than be on

recover *(re kuver)* what secretaries do to incriminating documents that have been uncovered

Red China *(red chi ne)* what the First Lady serves dinner on at the White House

red tape *(red tap)* the invisible material that holds the government together

reform *(ri form)* an attempt to get right what was screwed up the first time

register *(rej e ster)* a device in a supermarket which George Bush did not know how to use

regulation *(reg ye la shen)* what Ronald Reagan hopes to achieve by eating more bran

rejected *(re jekt ed)* what the voters of Massachusetts seem unwilling to do

Religious Right *(Ri lijes Rit)* people who are religious and always think they're right

repeal *(ri pel)* what Ronald Reagan sometimes tries to do to a banana

Republican *(Ri pub li ken)* someone who believes in family values ... unless the family in question isn't valuable enough

results *(re zultz)* insults that are repeated over and over again

retreat *(ri tret)* a place where politicians go to get away from getting away from things

revolution *(rev e loo shen)* what your head makes upon hearing the dumb things politicians says

rights *(ritz)* what Bob Dole will never hit you with

Roe vs. Wade *(Ro vs. Wad)* what stupid politicians think your options are when stranded in the water

run off *(run off)* what all politicians do at the mouth

scandal *(skan dl)* the result of a politician getting caught at what he normally does everyday

Secret Service *(se krit sûr vis)* what hookers give politicians during late night rendezvous

self-govern *(self guv ern)* what governors do when they're alone and horny

share *(shâr)* who stupid congressmen think Sonny Bono was married to

shelters *(shel terz)* what Republicans want to close unless their taxes are in one

shut-down *(shut doun)* when government workers are ordered not to work as opposed to when they simply don't work on their own

signature *(sig ne cher)* a scribble at the bottom of important documents often forged by a secretary

slap *(slap)* what crooked politicians get on the wrist and their supporters get in the face

Slick Willie *(slik wil e)* what Hillary checks Bill for when he's been out all night

smear tactics *(smer tak tiks)* what J. Edgar Hoover used to put on his make-up

Social Security *(so shel si kyoor ite)* a government program that is neither social nor secure

sound bite *(sound bit)* what President Clinton can take out of a Big Mac™

speech *(spech)* something delivered to the American people even though none of us ordered one

speed limit *(sped lim it)* according to Marion Barry, about two grams a night

spin doctor *(spin dok ter)* one who hides the political message so those who might hear it don't get sick

staff meeting *(stäf meting)* what gay politicians have in the men's room

stagnation *(stag na shen)* what the country would be if no one could find a date

status quo *(sta te kwo)* just as bad

straw poll *(strô pol)* a poll as believable as the material it is named after

stumping *(stump ing)* what you do to politicians when you ask a simple question

subsidy *(sub si de)* what Dan Quayle thinks is something less than a city

succession *(sek sesh en)* what Bob Packwood tried to get young girls to engage in

supply side economics *(se pli sid eke nom ikz)* where you supply the government with everything you have until there is nothing left on your side

supporter *(se pôr ter)* what FDR needed or else he'd fall down

tax cut *(taks kut)* a tax increase that's simply not as high as they told you it would be

taxing *(taks ing)* what your day is compared to a politicians

term *(tûrm)* the length of time it takes for people to realize a politician is incompetent

term limits *(tûrm lim itz)* what Dan Quayle has in regard to his vocabulary

"the button" *(The But n)* what The President can put his finger on to give the First Lady an orgasm

The Great Depression *(The Grat Di Presh En)* what Janet Reno feels after looking in the mirror. "And the moment Miss Reno looked in the mirror, The Great Depression began."

"the left" *(the left)* the only hand which Bob Dole can write with

think tank *(thingk tangk)* a tank which, in Washington, would be empty

third party *(thurd pärte)* where politicians go after the 2nd party ends

third place *(thûrd plas)* where Hillary doesn't let Bill put his slick willie

three martini lunch *(thre mär te ne lunch)* what Ted Kennedy has after a three martini breakfast

thumbs up *(thumz up)* what voters can find in politician's butts

TIME™ *(Tim)* a) a magazine that reports on political issues b) what it didn't take much of to count Michael Dukakis' votes

tourism *(toor iz em)* a disease suffered by those who give tours of the White House

trade deficit *(trad def e cit)* the result of a politician's inability to trade insults with another politician

traditionalist *(tre dish e nl ist)* one who believes in screwing things up the old fashioned way

trickle down *(trik el doun)* a) what Ronald Reagan thought money could do b) what Ronald Reagan's memories now do

Tricky Dick *(trike dik)* what Richard Nixon was and what Bob Packwood has

UN *(Yoo En)* what politicians ask each other before getting involved in a cover up

unclear *(un kler)* the color of a Marion Barry urine sample

undecided *(un di sid id)* what Ted Kennedy is when given a glass of bourbon and a glass of scotch

underdog *(under dôg)* where someone would be if they were under Janet Reno

underground *(un der ground)* a) a political faction opposing a government b) where Richard Nixon is

understands *(un der stanz)* where most of Washington's illegal dealings take place

unemployed *(un emploid)* what social workers would be if they were really good at their jobs

Unknown Soldier *(Un non sol jer)* the guy who took Bill Clinton's place in Viet Nam

uphill *(up hil)* where Clarence Thomas allegedly wanted to go

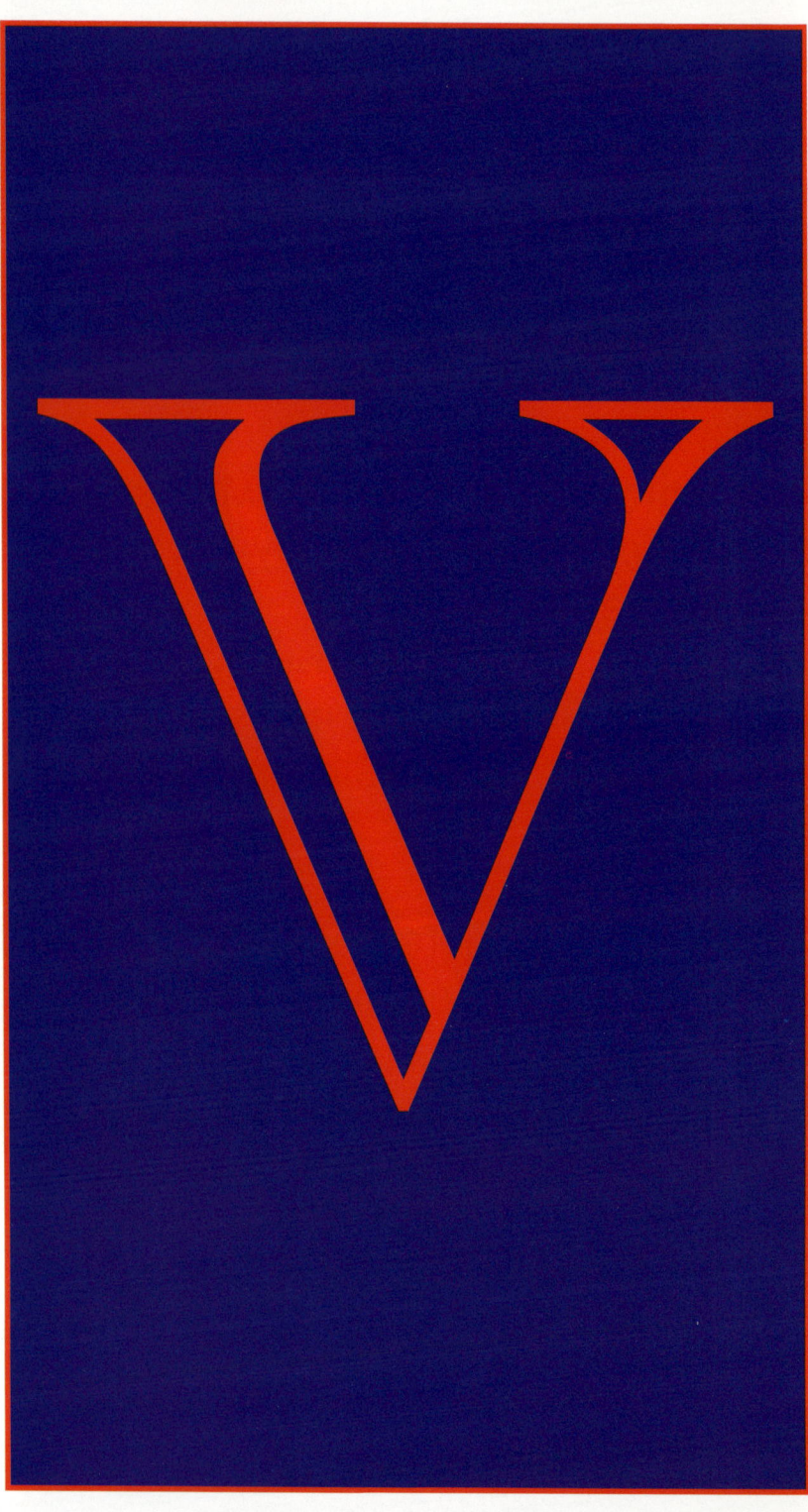

veterans *(vet er enz)* what all politicians are in regard to lying and cheating

veto *(vito)* the name of someone who will never hold the office of the President

victory *(vik te re)* what politicians always claim even in defeat

vision *(vizh en)* what George Bush wishes he didn't have when Barbara comes into the bedroom

voters *(vo terz)* those people fooled into thinking their one ballot can actually make a difference

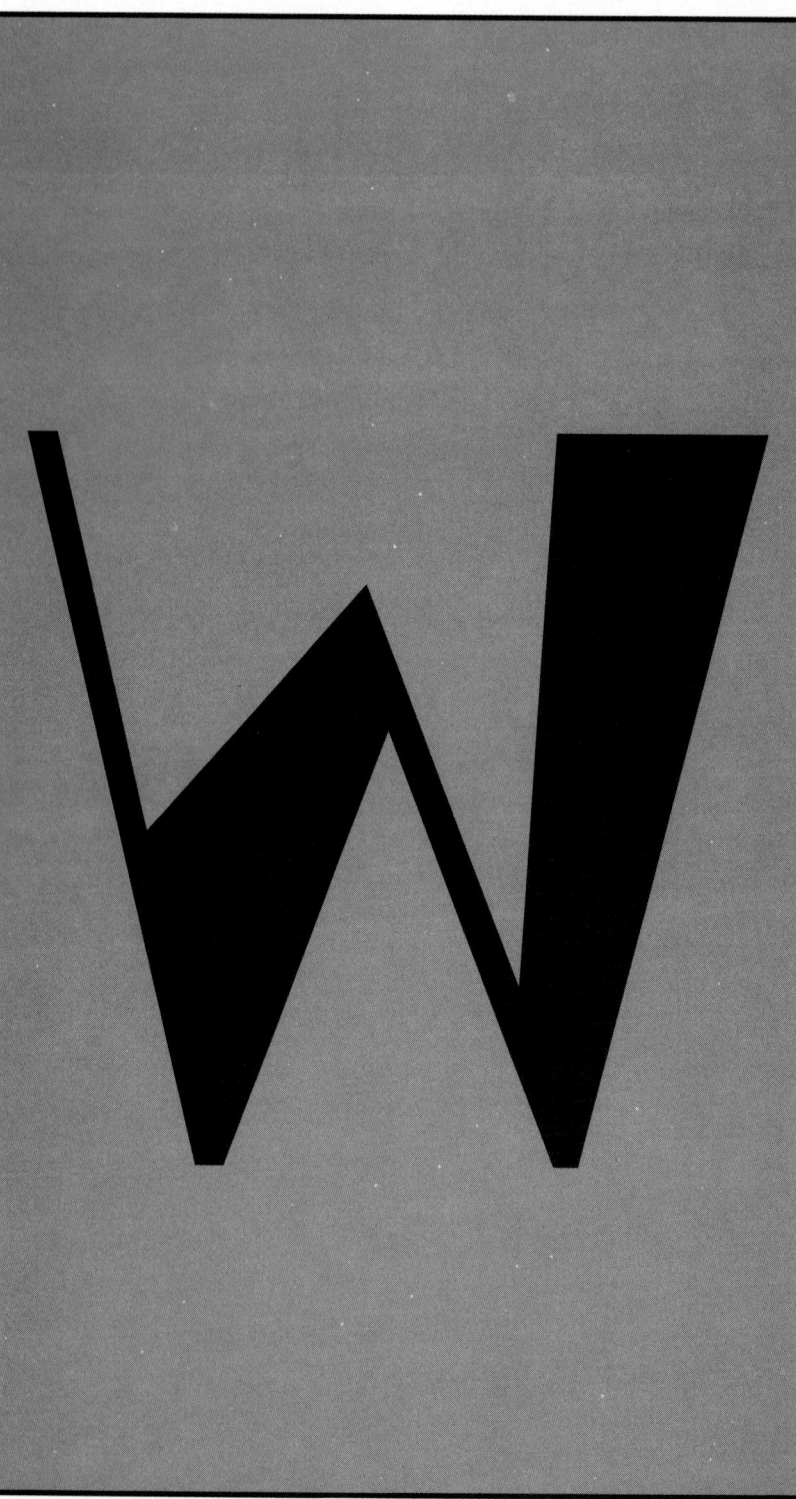

wallet *(wôl it)* what JFK and Marilyn had to do when a bed wasn't available

Washington Monument *(Wosh ing ten Mon ey ment)* what George Washington used to show the ladies in bed

waste *(wast)* the only thing government is efficient at producing

well-grounded *(wel grounded)* what Chelsea Clinton is when caught sneaking boys into her room

Whitewater *(wit water)* What David Duke prefers to drink

withdraw *(with drô)* what LBJ couldn't do from Viet Nam and JFK didn't want to do from Marilyn Monroe

work *(wurk)* what you do to help support those who don't

X *(eks)* the letter politicians look for when signing documents they haven't even read

X-Ray *(eks ra)* what many politicians think is a form of pig latin

yawn *(yôn)* the direct result of watching C-SPAN

year *(yer)* a period of time in which Washington can accomplish absolutely nothing

yes man *(yes man)* a) someone who always agrees with their superior b) the response when asked if Michael Dukakis was a loser

Z